What I Didn't Give to Goodwill

poems by

Ginger Graziano

Finishing Line Press
Georgetown, Kentucky

What I Didn't Give to Goodwill

for Jennifer and Jeremy, Declan, and Don

ACKNOWLEDGMENTS

My gratitude goes to the editors of the following journals in which some of
the poems in this book, sometimes in earlier versions, first appeared.

American Journal of Poetry: What I Didn't Give to Goodwill; Night Ride
Amethyst Review: The Garden in April
Front Porch Review: Monday, 6am, Driving
Great Smokies Review: Awakening; For the Last Time; Fire; Sanctuary;
    The Pen
Kakalak: Flight; Light-Shocked Night; New Native Land
Sky Island Journal: On the Beach, Belmar, New Jersey
The Conium Review: Shed
The Sunlight Press: Bounty

Publisher: Leah Huete de Maines
Editor: Christen Kincaid
Cover Art: *Development* by Ginger Graziano
Author Photo: Don Eichmiller
Cover Design: Elizabeth Maines McCleavy

Order online: www.finishinglinepress.com
also available on amazon.com

Author inquiries and mail orders:
Finishing Line Press
PO Box 1626
Georgetown, Kentucky 40324
USA

Contents

JEREMY

What I Didn't Give to Goodwill

My son's baseball jacket with New York emblazoned
across the front. His football jacket, dark blue wool
with gold leather sleeves, left in the attic off his bedroom,
the hot smell of old wood trapped under the eaves.

Last month, I picked up his sneakers from the plastic bin
where I keep out-of-season shoes, the soles disintegrated
in my hands, just as our future became a bombed-out city
after the doctor gave us the verdict. All that was left
now was the faint impressions of his feet as if his shoes
had kept him on Earth,

I still wear, when I work in the garden, his old shirt,
sleeves rolled up, feeling the moisture between my fingers,
the soil's hidden world growing, unlike cells gone wild,
jammed against his closed skull, like overripe fruit,
tunneling deeper and deeper, devouring his life.

He wore the blue jacket in winter, hatless, ears red,
no gloves while I called, *put on a hat, it's freezing.*
He liked cold weather, his wavy hair, before it fell out,
blowing in the wind. He wore a baseball cap
to hide the crooked scar—a backward C on the right side
of his head, like a gruesome beast had wounded him
mortally.

Tall and determined, he strode into the morning,
headed for high school, not wanting to be a sissy.
Already separated from his friends, his life detoured,
headed for a dark cliff as I watched.

When I reach into the closet, my breath falters, I bury
my nose in his jacket but his scent is long gone.
I remember his just-washed hair clean and fresh or salty
from the beach, not those last months of chemo,
when he stunk of chemicals, like he'd drunk bleach.

When moths chew holes in his jackets,
I will see light through the broken threads.

Standing in the Doorway

October 28
The day started
at the hospital. Waiting.
The small routines: fresh water,
wiping his brow with a cool washcloth,
holding his hand. His heels cushioned
by pillows of blisters. *Rub my feet,*
he would say before the coma.

He had a few spoonfuls
of Maureen's soup, anointing his
parched lips, then drifted to the between
world, turning from us. *Look for the light,*
I whispered in his ear. He moaned.
Don't stay here! It's OK to go,
in case he felt a son's responsibility.

Laura, his favorite nurse, checked his vitals.
A few more hours.
Ten of us stood around his bed,
silent sentinels. I put my hand on his heart,
sent all my love into that touch.

The room quiet as a temple.
We listened for his breath, a slowing rhythm.
My fear that death might be violent
or a struggle, but his was a fire going
out.

Slips of Paper

Platelet count yesterday 36.
Dilantin level 15. Both good.
It's night.
I'm staying tonight.
Try to sleep for a little bit.
This is some medicine to relax you.
I will not let them hurt you.
The chemo did it.
We think your hearing will get better.
I will be with you.
We'll try everything.

Smaller pieces of chicken?
Tell Jenny what?
We'll have Thanksgiving soon.
Who do you want to invite?
I'm getting the juice.
I love you.

Look at me. You are very sick.
I can't make you better.
The cancer is growing.
You will not be in pain.

Last Night Home

I break my son out of the hospital, a giddy ride
through Manhattan to score corned beef, whatever
he wants, drive across the Triboro Bridge, sun setting
over the Towers.

He enters our house on Littleworth Lane: we pretend
he can inhabit an earlier memory of peace and laughter.
But he's just visiting, saying goodbye before he leaves
for good. So little

I can do except this gesture, this 24-hour escape,
as if we can fly away, ascend into a different story, but
here we are, walking into the living room
where our birds chirp hello. What must

he feel like to enter this parallel world that moves unaware
while he lingers, suspended. I cook his favorite foods
like I always do, watch him eat and eat—eating life,
sucking it up.

He's exhausted, too weak to climb the stairs, rests
on my bed. I have work deadlines pressing, but fuck it,
I toss them aside to lie beside him, listening to his breath
all night, sleep not what I need.

The dog snores lightly, red maple outside the window
sheds leaves. I pray morning won't come, that maybe
the sun—that leering eye, that fickle presence,
that heat-blasted dream destroyer—forgets to get up,
sleeps late so we can remain in this cocoon of normal.
But slowly the sky hints at dawn:
a searchlight coming to find us.

Night Ride

Tony brings the car around.
Glenda and I get in,
windows closed against the chill.
No one talks about Jeremy,
my dying son we just visited
in the hospital.

Not much traffic at 11pm.
Lights turn red, then green. We blast
through smoke rising from manholes.
Ambulances roar past bleating, flashing.
A half moon shines
over the East River Drive.

One of us says something
not even funny. Our laughter starts
like a hiccup that won't be scared away,
from the pit below our guts
where dead things fester.

Howls ricochet off the windows.
We are screaming, gasping,
a wheezy calliope squeezed,
monkey on our shoulders banging cymbals,
helpless to stop.

The Pen

At my son's hospital room, a dim glow
backlights him so he floats out of the shadows.
He's still awake at ten pm, sitting up in bed,
paper and pen spread on the crumpled covers.

The bed sinks under my weight till we're at eye level.
What are the papers? His eyes search mine.
The doctor brought them. What should I do?
I draw my breath in.

Rummage for answers. None come. The pen waits,
as if our deepest feelings could change the outcome,
as if the papers could fly out the window to join
the falling leaves.

Traffic's distant honk, his beeping heart monitor.
His hands on the white sheet outline his legs and feet.
I look at his bald head, swollen scrunched up face,
his trusting eyes.

He held me when my father died, no words,
just his comforting arms, and I thought, how blessed I am
to have mothered this loving soul, never thinking
this was our future.

Jeremy, I don't know what's on the other side,
but I'd want to either live or die, not be lost in a coma.
We both feel your grandpa close now.
Ma, he's like a warm blanket cocooning me.

He pauses to take this in, picks up the pen and in his shaky
handwriting, signs the order not to resuscitate.

Sanctuary

Jeremy orders popcorn, cookies, doughnuts,
enough for a large party but it's just the two
of us. We'll never eat all of this.
Then I think, so what?

We lie on his hospital bed, watching
Fire in the Sky, eating everything,
holding hands. His nurses stop by
to comment on our feast.
The comfort of our love—
even here.

Near the end, bald and beautiful, face lit
from within—he's already partly gone.
Hand on his heart, I kiss him goodbye,
tell him to look for the light,
Poppy is waiting.

My Sea Cliff—a place of refuge after
his death to wander late at night
with the moon's light shimmering
on the harbor, to hug pine trees,
their bark rough against my cheek—
stand-ins for family who are gone.

Porches with people murmuring
and laughing, far from city streets,
loud traffic, and stress. Solace of wind
chimes, houses aglow in the dark
invite me to come alive again, let
peace enter my starved heart.

The Fire That Can't Go Out

The kindling folds
in upon itself
paper melts
turns black along
its edges as flames
grab and suck
for air, flick
their tongues for more

My son's brain
tumor information
igniting—
stage 4 glioblastoma
uncontrollable rage
aggressive astrocytoma
screaming fury
surgeries, chemotherapy
radiation, headaches
seizures, Dilantin
platelet infusions
my beautiful son
ashen, shrunken

Snow falls
like endless grief…
I give up shoveling a path
to the woodpile,
stack wood on the porch
every night…

My ritual—get wine
pour a glass
make fire—
feed it rolled-up
magazines, receipts
from Sloan-Kettering
hospital crumpled

and tossed—
these, I can destroy

Every night wind
blows into this house
with no insulation
as I huddle close
to the fire's temporary
warmth

The wood glows
with fire's life, pulsing
until it too is
reduced to ash.

BEFORE

Genealogy

I'm from Ellis Island immigrants
lower East Side Italian grandparents
who died while last century was still young.
From stories my father didn't tell
about the orphanage years.
From my mother's childhood in Bayonne's Flats
with exploding gas storage tanks.

From aunts and uncles walking dusty country roads,
my mother's worry and my father's anxiety
etched in the frown between his eyes.
From before cell phones and computers,
when my father's old car had a rumble seat.

I'm from the sauce pot bubbling on the stove,
my Uncle Tom's homemade wine,
bird song and flower seeds,
church and rosary beads, my father's
whistle and his long thin face.

From maiden aunts' chocolate pudding,
card games and Scrabble, war factory jobs
and men who didn't come home.
Kruschikis and pierogies, spaghetti and meatballs.
Aunt Tessie's grape arbor, galumpkis and babushkas.

From my parents' cash they stashed behind
the refrigerator. Saved string and small dreams.
I'm from people who kept their mouths shut
and kept moving.

Vast

Mother stands at the edge
of the shore. All that water.
She can't swim. Her two children
are far out in deep water,
young and fearless. They laugh
as the looming wave breaks
and they disappear in the rush.
It races towards the beach, clatters
on the stones and broken shells.
Recedes.

The children rise from the foam,
look at her raised arm, furiously
pumping, come back.
The next wave is building height,
the sun glows through its long body,
thin rim of white water,
but this time, riding right to the top,
they see the length of the beach.

She has no power over
what enchants them.
The last remnants of the wave
tickle her feet. Sweat pours down
her armpits. Sun turns her skin
red. Daughter once again defies her,
son refuses to listen. Both of them
draw a line between what she wants
and where they are going.

On the Beach, Belmar, New Jersey

That first morning, my brother Jim and I bike
tree-filled streets to buy jelly donuts and eat them
at the boardwalk. Sun glints off breakers
that rise like cobras, curl and crash on the beach.
Water as far as we can see. No apartments to crowd
the view. Gulls careen overhead.
Our barefoot toes sink into sand as waves
beckon. *Deeper. Deeper.*

When my aunts and grandfather arrive, I retreat
to my own steamy attic bedroom. Privacy
an unheard-of luxury. Jim not snoring in the other bed.
None of his stinky underwear on the floor.

I strip to cool my sweaty skin. The mirror reveals
my naked hormone-flooded body. At the window,
salt breezes caress my budding breasts. My emotions
swirl like the dark clouds building outside.

That night the wind moans. I race to the beach
as the sea crashes over the miniature golf game
on the boardwalk. Over ocean-side streets.
Over porches and driveways. Rain lashes my body,
whips hair into my eyes. My gut churns, shocked
by the menacing face that arose like a wraith
from noon's calm water.

Nightmares haunt me when we return
to our suffocating Bronx apartment. I thrash
in sleep as waves suck me down. I wake in a sweat,
night after night. The ocean no longer beyond me,
but inside.

Awakening

Afterward, in his kitchen,
warm light streaming in,
he brings out the mango.

What is this? I ask,
when he holds it out.
I cup its heaviness,
surprised by its smooth
tight body, orange blush,
stem a protruding wick.

Does it taste like a peach?
He shakes his head,
peels the skin. Inside
a golden sun gleams.

You are like a child, he says,
just waking to the world.

Whose world? I say
as I grasp the mango,
the flesh sweet and rich,
all the way down to the pit.

Flight

We turn the dial to intercept
radio-transmitted words from the men
on the moon, as we speed through the Midwest
night, past houses aglow with families
watching the moonwalk. *One small step.*
Astronauts untethered from gravity hobble
in their bulky spacesuits, bounding over
lifeless craters.

We've traveled three days from New York.
Crossed the Hudson while the rising sun
turned the river as molten as our marriage
which smolders like a rancid cigarette.
Our unhappy cat wails from the backseat.
Nothing but space between us
as we rocket away from the ruins.

Our tiny capsule, stripped of all familiar
comforts except the tent, pots, stove,
sleeping bags that stuff the big-finned trunk
of our cheap Buick, a replacement we can afford
since we can't replace one another.

Through Pennsylvania's mountains
a month after the Cuyahoga caught fire—
polluted river as barren as the moon—
to Pittsburgh where two rivers join
to form the Ohio, past open fields, the moon
a thin fingernail in the dark sky.

There they were on that far-away surface,
until then virgin. Untouched.
Now tattooed with footprints. Later,
pictures of Earth, blue and cloud-draped—
a fragile radiant gem. Floating alone.
All of us together hurtling through darkness.

And here we are, determined to resuscitate
our crumbling marriage, headed
for California's sunlit promise, our footprints
all over the mess we had made.

Wild Black-Eyed Susans

Shock cut the cord of my tethered balloon, the day
my father died. I drifted aimlessly for months, dreading
the getaway my boss planned at his summer home
with my coworkers—the drawling Louisiana woman,
boyfriend skinny as a coconut tree, six-pack silent friend,
the tight-braided chirpy assistant, since the intimacy
of us packed in a cabin wasn't what I needed.
Grief, like an open wound that hadn't healed.

I drove with them from Manhattan, listening
to gossip about Bob Marley's recent cancer death,
Harry Chapin's fatal car crash, and then, just ahead,
a dead deer, looking like grief's muffled blanket,
strapped to the top of a red truck.

Vermont's pine-scented mountain air, like stepping
into a cool forest stream. That night, my boss's neighbor,
a gentle artist, sat next to me at the restaurant.
We ate salmon from each other's plates. I leaned
into his welcoming body, his mustache smile.
He offered to drive me back to the house. *Okay if we stop
at my loft first?* Yes, I said, slaloming back into my body,
alert against the car seat.

We veered off to his stone loft by the river. He poured me
a glass of wine, the moon glowed through the skylight,
his hand reached for mine. The string of my free-floating
balloon shuddered as he brought me back to solid ground.
Before we knew, the trees outside reclaimed their shapes
from the dark. *Wake up, I have to go.*

He dropped me at my boss's house where I gathered
a bouquet of tiger lilies and daises, remembering when
my father picked wild black-eyed Susans for me,
put them in my hand, saying, *Honey, these are for you.*
When first the skinny man and then the others woke,
saying, *You're up early,* I nodded as I arranged the flowers;
they were not a last goodbye but a strange new hello.

Shed

The skin contains echoes
    imitates a surface

the memory   the loss
 even still?
inside time crumbles   splits   melts
insistence drags back the hours   refuses to loosen its jaws

snake

              hisses
                coils
                    cells
                    pulse
            pinpoint
            eyes
            grab
              mine

this is the edge   the thin blade   the balance   the road ahead

the sun fades   the air is cool   I didn't need the scarf
place is a red square or black
life is a living thing or dead
the skull is white   smooth   unseeing
bone pure as sleep

have I stayed long enough?

tell me   I have forgotten the
stones and where they lead

AFTER

For the Last Time

When I drop my keys in the mailbox and tiptoe one last
time through the echoing rooms filled with the memory
of parties, healing ceremonies, friends left behind,
the lover who held me, my children gone—one south,
the other to his grave—and the unexpected comfort
of solitude,

When I leave this beloved town, with gratitude
for the years it sheltered me, and skirt the waterfront
by the dark bay alive with moonlight,

When I pass the towns where I raised my children alone,
remembering the love we created and how it nurtured us
through the hard years,

When I drive familiar roads past my birthplace,
where I walked city streets wondering
how to create a dream from the empty sky,

When I cross the Hudson in the rain and gaze
at the jeweled lights snaking along the shoreline
to the end of the island where the towers glow
and fill the sky until they are swallowed in the clouds,

When I have nothing but what I carry in my car
and the voice inside repeats, *you're done*,
and I know this to be true,

Then I am free.

Ashes

Here on my porch, surrounded
by trees—my new friends—birds swoop
like careening feathered planes.
Greetings trill, tweet, caw, praise
me for having left the city noise
and subways, dirt and crowds.

The new kitchen cabinets
are stacked on my living room floor
like horizontal skyscrapers. I'm dancing
to Stevie Wonder's *Songs in the Key of Life*
when Lainie calls,

"They fell" is all she says.
"What fell?"
*"The Towers, two planes flew
into them."*

My television not yet connected,
I drive to the only place I know in Asheville
with a TV, Hannah Flanagan's. Walk into the bar.
The few regulars sip their beers,
not even looking at the TV.
The Towers explode over and over,
fall straight down to the earth.

I order wine. Order more wine,
a pack of Marlboros even though
I no longer smoke. I smoke them,
every last cigarette, hot smoke rising
as I watch them fall.

Replanted

I left family and friends, both living and dead in New York,
my son buried in the welcoming earth, drove
a hatchback crammed with cuttings from the garden
to my new life, Tony's third-generation irises,
Jerry's two buckets of perennials.

My mother could grow African violets from a leaf
pressed into soil. My father picked wild
Black-eyed Susans for me as a child. Now
mine flourish among bee balm, tiger lilies,
and sochan from the Cherokee.

Peggy gifted the first trillium, which has grown into
a community under the pieris. Carolina wrens and robins
build nests, birth babies, bring nestlings to feast
on abundant insects. Bats, butterflies, bees and squirrels
make a home like I've done.

The lily from Don for our anniversary has eight blooms
each July. I wear Jeremy's green-striped shirt when I dig
and plant, sleeves smeared with dirt. The tiny red Japanese
maple from Jennifer for Mother's Day twenty years ago,
expanded to fill the space, like a flaming heart.

Light-Shocked Night

Milky Way caught in the web
        of naked tree branches
                star ornaments
Jemez Mountains   3AM
      Valle Grande
        caldera of an ancient volcano

        Twenty miles of empty
           Filled with shadow   Wind whistles
             sounds echo into far depths
             Elk bugle   coyotes howl
Such bitter beauty

Standing on the edge
        questions blow away

Did you come here seeking relief?
        To empty your own vessel of sorrow?
It is empty
        It may never be empty

        Hold out the fired bowl of your heart
      Catch the moment
Face into the swirling wind
    Let Earth succor you
        Every minute a new awe

    Your scoured center fills with wild night   eons deep

      when all else is gone
        welcome
      Death's opposite face

Monday, 6am, Driving

Porch lights glimmer like glowworms.
A lone kitchen light already on.
Someone's brewing coffee, swallowing comfort.

Solitary man walks his dog,
jogger passes, ponytail swinging—
a pendulum keeping time.

I love the hour before night shakes off
its velvet cloak and stretches, before
imagination fades like melting snow.

And yet, black tree shapes looming
on the horizon resemble a tsunami's silent
approach. Low down, between dark clouds,
a faint glow hints at dawn's promise—
a respite from this chaotic world.

Fires, floods, breakdowns, war.
Glaciers melt, refugees search for safety.
Three friends on chemo.

I grip the steering wheel as I cross
the swollen French Broad—a wild ribbon
filled with broken trees, devouring its banks
like the first mouthfuls of doom.

At the Y, warm water surrounds and soothes
as I circle the pool, backstroking towards dawn.
My brain counts laps instead of imminent
destruction. Ceiling skylights morph—
inky black   ashy gray   misty blue.
The rhythm of rippling water
drops me back into my body,
which will end but not this morning.

The Garden in April

Nature shows that survival is a practice
Wintering by Katherine May

This spring: fits and starts. The joy of the first field
of crocus, white candytuft on dried lawn glows
like a beacon. A hint of green, a smatter of tiny buds.
Too early, I lament. Like a merry-go-round coming back
to the brass ring: a reset—one night of cold wind,
freezing rain and nature cycles back. Pears, magnolias
go brown. Winter triumphant again. But new growth,
unstoppable. Warm sun and cool nights toughen.

I watch the garden's teaching as I move through surgery
and slow recovery. Now Japanese maple's red leaves form
a scrim pattern in front of the weeping cherry, still bright
with blossoms. Six days past surgery I wake to lazy
snowflakes drifting earthward. Another reset.
But the garden's promise spurs me on.

Bounty

The skate park—a spray-painted canvas
of graffiti, skateboarders swooshing
on cement waves—nestled
in the Blue Ridge Mountains.

Some fall, spring back, jump over
obstacles. I'm reminded of my last few
years—one surgery after another,
healing, recovering—only
to relapse with the next one.

Nearby, standing at a rickety table,
a young woman wearing a Dolphins
baseball cap, ripped jeans, faded
sweatshirt beckons, *We have two pounds
of steamed oysters from the coast.* I pry
open a gritty rippled shell with a knife.

Glistening morsel revealed like Venus
rising from the sea. Drop succulent meat
into my mouth. Unexpected rush
of salt, like diving into the waves.
I am eating the briny sea.

Memories of pacing the beach to gather
strength after being broken by loss,
the rhythm of the surf like a primal heartbeat,
calmed me. In the distance, surfers rose on
mountainous waves, to be delivered
to the beach, undaunted.

New Native Land

Jim is wheeled up the ramp at Savannah's airport,
one year past his stroke. Lynn carries
what he can't anymore—the ranch, the daily work
caretaking the animals, chores that never end.
Spanish moss's tan tinsel drips from live oaks
like braided dreadlocks, swaying.

Waiting for ice cream at Leopold's, his tired feet
propped on a chair, we chat—words chosen slowly
take new paths to reach his lips. The temporary
house till they sell the ranch, according to him,
is freedom.

At Lulu's, drunk on chocolate, we eat our way through
the stress of eleven months, when Jim's mind
was caught in a groove like a looping record unable
to jump free, free, free. Would he come back to us?
And here he is, defying limits as usual.

He leans on his cane at Tybee Island, shuffles up
the wooden ramp towards the ocean, his face transfixed
in the breeze as the sea breathes life into him. Blows
him kisses. Sea grass waves. Gulls weave. Grackles cackle.

He remembers our Belmar vacations, riding our bikes
as fast as the wind to get jelly donuts. Eat them
at the boardwalk. The waves drop and embrace the earth
briefly before receding into the vast sea
that sparkles in front of us.

Ethiopian Coptic Cross

I press against her skin, right above her heart.

What made her choose me in the jewelry shop
in Heraklion, Crete? She didn't plan to buy anything.

I'm not a delicate gold necklace, elegant or formal. No,
I'm a silver coptic cross, diamond-shaped with four birds,
hinged with a circle in the middle. Wholeness.

She stares at me in wonder. Puts me on a silver chain thick
as a rope, wears me all the time, like another limb,
feels naked without me.

I have a long history going back to Africa.
And the years I've been with her, her friends, this poem,
her painting. Her doubts, her big heart.
I've witnessed it all.

I gleam from the constant touching, like to be admired,
out in the world, traveling to many countries. I watched
when she met her husband. As her grandson slipped
out of her daughter.

Strangers approach, ask about me. Men as well as women.
A conversation opener, a story filled with laughter,
Imbued with her essence, an eye drawing people in,
heart to heart.

Come Out
for Don

Come out. The moon rises like a tropical tangerine,
dripping light across our dappled porch.

It's easy to curl up safe inside but remember
when we crawled from the tent as coyotes' crooned
love songs. Our hair rose with our bodies;
branches tattooed our faces blue gray.
A possum toddled the path, led by her nose.

Come out. Let's dance in the meadow's rippling breath,
chase our long shadows. Toss blue shawls
over our heads. Shed clothes in moon glow.
Turn feral as young lovers, filling the sky with endless
vistas, sizzling brighter than an incandescent galaxy.
The North Star guides us as we walk blind at night,
mist-bathed in cool delight, feet faultlessly
feeling our way.

Wake up. Let's crawl into the dark again,
tiptoe past sleepers to drive roads unlit,
stars like freckles on God's nose.

Born and raised in New York City, **Ginger Graziano** studied at Hunter College and graduated from Kean College with a BA in Fine Arts. While raising her children, Jennifer and Jeremy, as a single mother, she worked in Manhattan as a graphic designer at IBM and design director for children's educational publishers. She moved to Asheville, North Carolina, in 2001 having fallen in love with the mountains. She created Ginger Graziano Design Group with regional and national clients.

She met her husband, Don, hiking and they have travelled around North America, Europe and New Zealand, on hiking adventures. Her children have been a source of delight, and her grandson Declan is an unexpected gift later in life. As a author, poet, sculptor and painter, her creativity has blossomed like her garden.

Her poems have been published in *The American Journal of Poetry, Kakalak, Sky Island Journal, Rockvale Review, The Sunlight Press, The Great Smokies Review,* among others. Chapters from her memoir *See, There He Is*, published in 2015, were featured in *Stone Voices* and *Embodied Effigies*.

Her art show Full Circle: Conversations in Art and Poetry was exhibited at *Pink Dog Creative* in Asheville's River Arts District June-July 2024

Explore her creative pursuits at *www.gingergraziano.com*

www.ingramcontent.com/pod-product-compliance
Lightning Source LLC
Chambersburg PA
CBHW022048080426
42734CB00009B/1278